# Jobs If You Like...

# Sport

Charlotte Guillain

**www.raintreepublishers.co.uk**
Visit our website to find out
more information about
Raintree books.

**To order:**
☎ Phone 0845 6044371
▤ Fax +44 (0) 1865 312263
▣ Email myorders@raintreepublishers.co.uk

Customers from outside the UK please telephone +44 1865 312262

Raintree is an imprint of Capstone Global Library
Limited, a company incorporated in England and
Wales having its registered office at 7 Pilgrim Street,
London, EC4V 6LB – Registered company number:
6695582

Edited by Rebecca Rissman, Daniel Nunn, and
Adrian Vigliano
Designed by Steve Mead
Picture research by Elizabeth Alexander
Originated by Capstone Global Library
Printed and bound in China by South China Printing
Company

ISBN 978 1 406 24072 6 (hardback)
16 15 14 13 12
10 9 8 7 6 5 4 3 2 1

**British Library Cataloguing in Publication Data**
[select]
A full catalogue record for this book is available from
the British Library.

**Acknowledgements**
We would like to thank the following for permission to
reproduce photographs: [select]

Cover photograph of [select] reproduced with
permission of [select].

We would like to thank [name of organization or
individual] for [pronoun] invaluable help in the
preparation of this book.

Every effort has been made to contact copyright
holders of material reproduced in this book. Any
omissions will be rectified in subsequent printings if
notice is given to the publisher.

**Disclaimer**
All the Internet addresses (URLs) given in this book were
valid at the time of going to press. However, due to
the dynamic nature of the Internet, some addresses
may have changed, or sites may have changed or
ceased to exist since publication. While the author and
publisher regret any inconvenience this may cause
readers, no responsibility for any such changes can be
accepted by either the author or the publisher.

# Contents

Some words are shown in bold, **like this**. You can find out what they mean by looking in the glossary.

# Why does sport matter?

Do you love playing sport? Or maybe you enjoy watching sport? Even if it's not your favourite activity, sport is important for all of us. Exercise keeps us fit and healthy and can help us to relax and enjoy ourselves.

Sport is a great way to have fun.

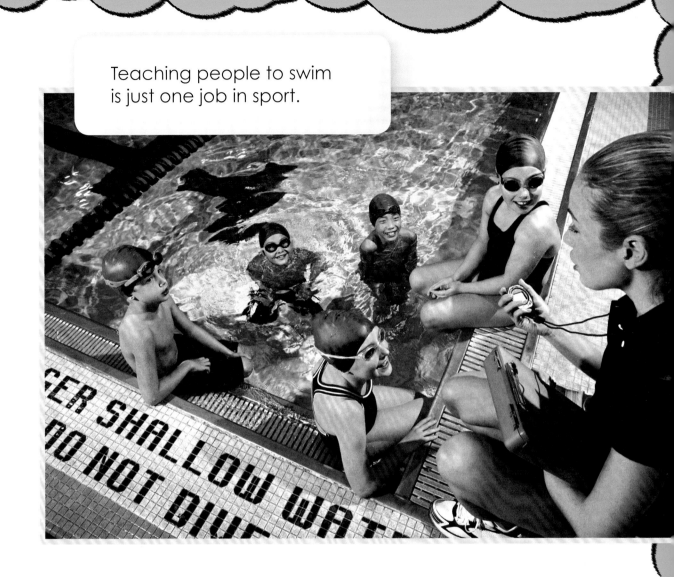

Teaching people to swim is just one job in sport.

If you like exercising then you might like to get a job that involves sport. Read this book to find out about some great sports jobs. Could one of them be for you?

# e a sports coach

If you were a sports coach, your job would be to teach people how to exercise safely and play well. Some sports coaches work with children who are learning a sport. Other sports coaches work with **professional** sportsmen and women.

Sports coaches need to help a team work together.

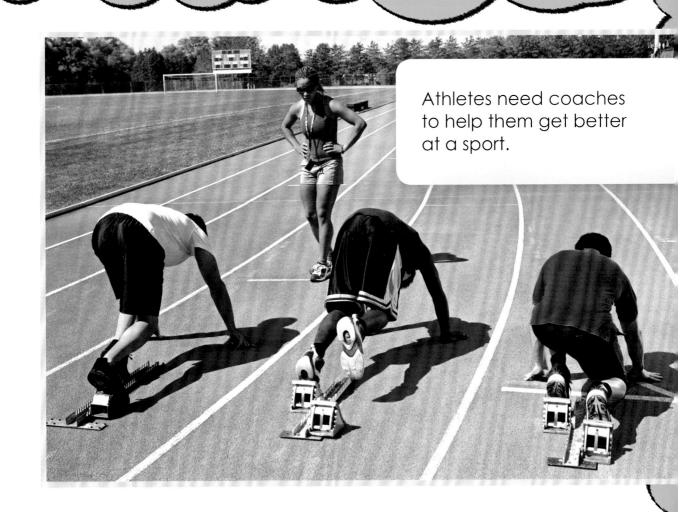

Athletes need coaches to help them get better at a sport.

Sports coaches help people to stay fit and learn the skills they need for a sport. They make sure people know the rules and play a game fairly. Coaches also help to **motivate** people. They tell people when they are doing well and what they can do to improve.

# Be a sports psychologist

If you were a sports psychologist, your job would be to look at how sport changes the way people think and feel. You would work with a team or athlete and help them to play or **perform** better.

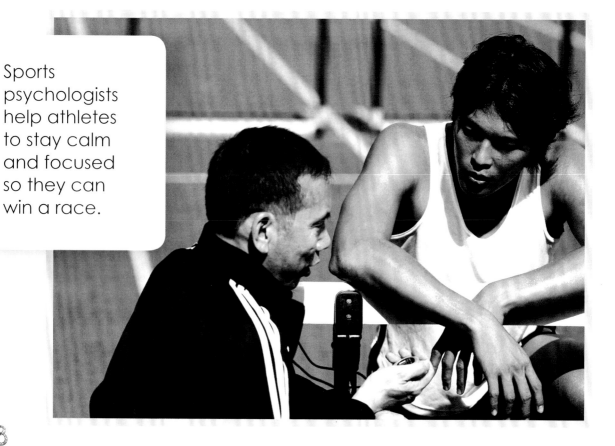

Sports psychologists help athletes to stay calm and focused so they can win a race.

Sports psychologists can help sportsmen and women manage when they have to do a lot of training. They help to keep people positive if they are injured. Sports psychologists help people to set new goals and work towards them.

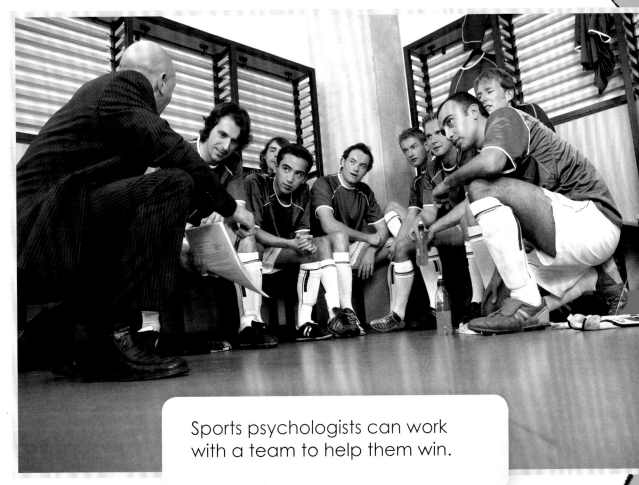

Sports psychologists can work with a team to help them win.

# Be a sports equipment designer

If you were a sports **equipment** designer, you would look at ways to make equipment better and safer. Some designers make swimwear that helps people to swim faster. Others design snowboards that win competitions and look great!

New snowboards are being designed all the time.

This cyclist's helmet helps him to cycle faster.

Sports equipment designers usually **specialize** in one sport. They might use science to understand how equipment can make someone faster. They use computers to help them design new gear.

# a personal trainer

If you were a personal trainer, you would help people to exercise and become fit. You would work out a special training programme for a person and help them to follow it.

Personal trainers push people to exercise more than they did before.

Personal trainers encourage and support people as they exercise.

Personal trainers have to get to know each person they work with. They make sure their training programme is right for them. They might give people advice on food and health.

# Be a fitness instructor

If you were a fitness instructor, you might work at a sports or leisure centre. You would give people instructions as they exercise. Some fitness instructors teach yoga or show people how to use **equipment** in a gym.

Some fitness instructors teach aerobics or keep fit classes.

Fitness instructors need to be fit and healthy to show people how to exercise. They need to check everyone in their class is well enough to exercise. Fitness instructors need to be energetic and good at giving instructions clearly.

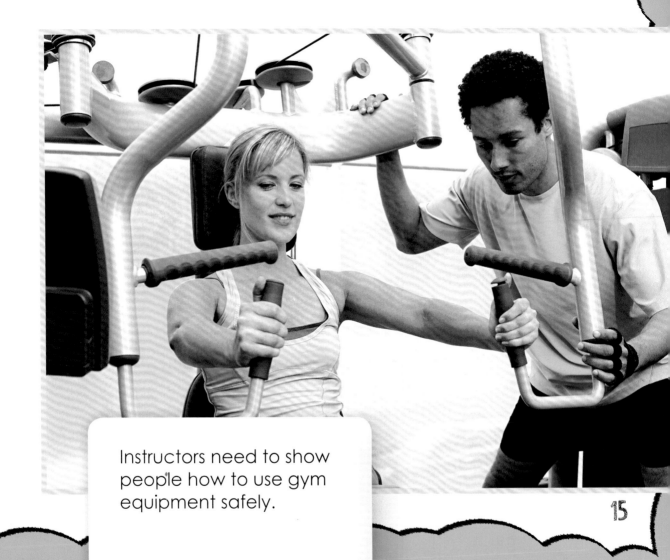

Instructors need to show people how to use gym equipment safely.

# Be a sports development officer

If you were a sports development officer, your job would be to make sure many people can exercise and play sport. You would talk to people who don't exercise and encourage them to get fit. You might organize new sports activities to get more people involved.

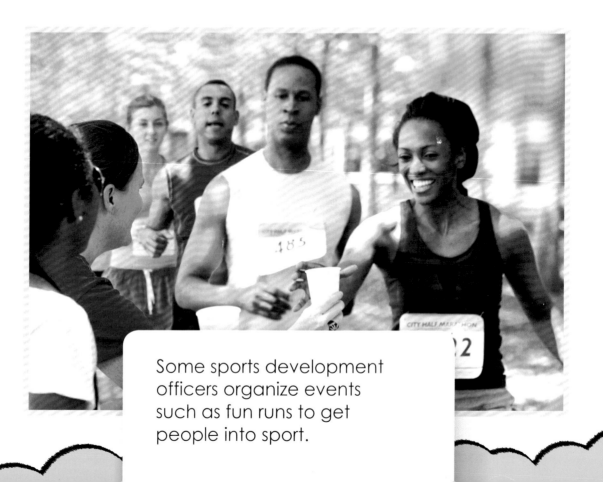

Some sports development officers organize events such as fun runs to get people into sport.

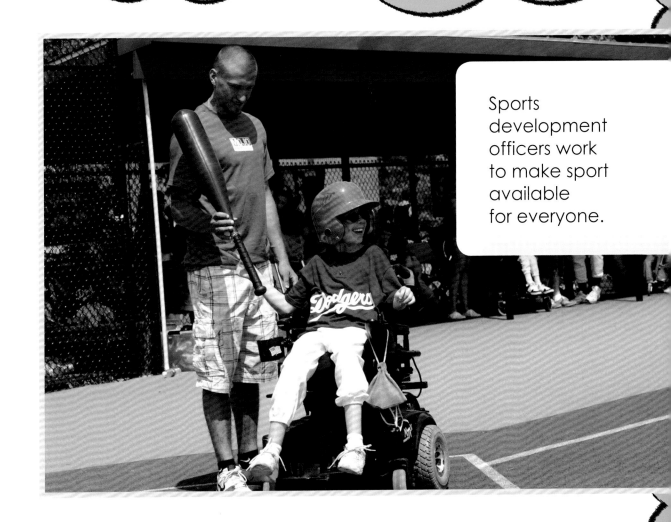

Sports development officers work to make sport available for everyone.

Many sports development officers work with children and young people who need to exercise. Some work with disabled people to help them take part in the sports that interest them. They have to organize a team of coaches and **volunteers**.

# Be a dancer

If you are doing well in dance classes, maybe you could be a **professional** dancer. Some dancers **perform** ballet and others enjoy modern or ballroom dance. Some dancers work in a theatre while others dance on television or in music videos.

Professional ballet dancers have to train hard for many years.

Dance groups practise hard to make sure they move well together.

Dancers have to work very hard to stay fit, strong, and flexible. They follow a **choreographer's** instructions to learn special dance moves. Dancers have to be good at remembering their routines and working together as a team.

# e an occupational therapist

If you were an occupational therapist, you would help people with **physical** or **mental** problems. You would suggest ways for your patients to cope with everyday life. You might use sport and other activities to help your patients feel better.

Exercise can help people recover after accidents.

Occupational therapists talk to a patient to find out what he or she needs. Then they make a programme for the patient to follow. Occupational therapists help to keep their patients active and positive.

Yoga can help people with physical and mental illnesses to relax.

# Be a sports professional

If you are very good at a sport, you might be able to do it for your job. A sports **professional** is someone who is able to earn the money they need to live by **competing** in their sport.

Only the very best athletes and players can be professional.

Sports professionals have to spend a lot of time training. They need to eat healthy food and work with doctors and coaches to stay fit. They often have to travel to go to competitions and **perform** well under pressure.

Sports professionals have to play in front of many people.

# Be a sports journalist

If you like watching sport, then you might like to be a sports journalist. Your job would be to watch matches and competitions and report on them. You might write about sport for a newspaper or website, or you might talk about sport on television.

Sports journalists need to talk to the people who play sport.

Sports writers have to write about a match or competition in an exciting way. They need to understand the sport very well to tell people what happened. Sports reporters on television often talk about sport as it is happening.

Often sports reporters help to explain how a sport is played.

# Choosing the right job for you

When you decide what you want to do when you grow up, don't just think about school subjects. Think about what you enjoy doing. If you like to be active every day then maybe you could be a fitness instructor or coach.

If you like to help people then perhaps you could be an occupational therapist. If you like writing then you might like to be a sports journalist. There are so many exciting jobs that use sport that there is something to suit everyone.

## Five things you couldn't do without sport

- Keep fit and healthy
- Watch matches on television
- Ride your bike
- Go swimming
- Dance with your friends

# Sport job chart

If you want to find out more about any of the jobs in this book, start here:

| | Dancer | Fitness instructor | Occupational therapist | Personal trainer | |
|---|---|---|---|---|---|
| **You need to:** | Be an excellent dancer | Be fit and active | Be good at problem solving | Be able to see what different people need | |
| **Best thing about it:** | Doing what you love every day! | It's fun! | Helping a patient do something for themselves! | Helping people reach their goals! | |

| | Sports coach | Sports development officer | Sports equipment designer | Sports journalist | Sports professional | Sports psychologist |
|---|---|---|---|---|---|---|
| | Be good at **motivating** people | Be good at finding out what people need | Have good design ideas | Know a lot about the rules of sport | Be outstanding in your sport | Be good at listening to people |
| | Seeing your players win! | Helping people to play the sport they want! | Seeing your **equipment** help someone win! | You get to watch sport all the time! | Winning! | Helping someone to be better at their sport! |

# Glossary

**choreographer**  person who plans and teaches dance steps and routines

**compete**  take part in a competition

**equipment**  item or items used to help someone do something

**mental**  to do with the mind

**motivate**  make people want to do something

**perform**  do something in front of other people

**physical**  to do with the body

**professional**  doing a job to earn money to live

**specialize**  to concentrate on one thing

**volunteer**  person who works for no money

# Find out more

**British Olympic Association**
www.olympics.org.uk/sports/
Find out more about different sports on
this website.

**Dance Kids**
www.dance-kids.org/
You can learn more about different types of
dance on this website.

# Index